This book is dedicated to the memory of Elvis Aron Presley

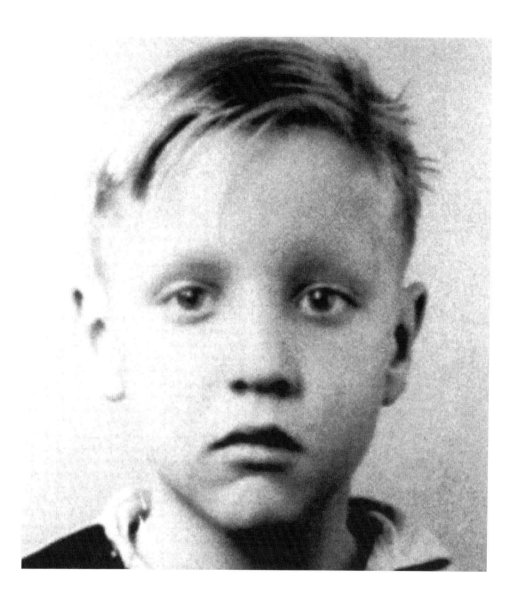

Contents

Elvis: king

To call Elvis the King of Rock and Roll, is to do him a disservice. He was much more than that. As a nickname, it makes for a good slogan and marketing tool, but it succeeds only in putting him into a restricted box that does not tell anything like the full story. Rock and Roll is merely one string to Elvis Presley's bow. He sang country, blues, gospel, pop, rock, Latin, and a whole array of unusual styles, particularly in his movies. So, those those tedious bores who proclaim cliches like 'Chuck Berry is the King of Rock and Roll' are presenting a petulant and meaningless argument.

People do not call Elvis The King because he was the first. People call Elvis The King because he was the best. Elvis himself refuted the nickname, humbly and sincerely saying that Fats Domino was the rightful owner of the title. But, in the end, it's simply a label that does not matter. What is great is great, with or without it.

Elvis Presley is the ultimate singer. An interpreter of song. In the same way an actor brings the character on the page to life, Elvis Presley brought everything that was needed to convey every word on the lyric sheet.

His biggest attributes were his sincerity and his inability to fake it. He was a man who seemingly had everything, yet could sing with complete believability that he had nothing. No matter what he sang, he could not hide his current state, be it elation, sadness or even disinterest.

When you hear Elvis sing, you are hearing the real deal. No auto tune, no trickery, just pure Elvis.

He may have fallen into the classic pitfalls of the rock and roll lifestyle, but when he stood in front of a microphone, all of those things ceased to matter and it was not simply a case of a

consummate professional – It was the real Elvis Presley.

Elvis: Actor

The idea that Elvis was a bad actor in bad films is a lazy surface opinion. A closer look would reveal that Elvis was in fact a brilliant actor who's true capabilities were rarely allowed to shine. Of course, many of his films did not warrant a Laurence Olivier level of performance, but whenever there was a challenge, Elvis rose to it. His first four films prior to his joining the army in 1958, showcased very good performances, particularly the last one, King Creole, in which he is superb. In this film, he plays Danny Fisher, a young man who is seemingly angry and lost. Elvis excels in every aspect in the portrayal of this character.

The quality of his films after his leaving the army, vary wildly. Some are excellent and others are a disgraceful waste of the man's abilities, to the eternal shame of all involved.

In Follow That Dream, 1962, Elvis plays a good hearted simpleton Toby Kwimper, and produced a brilliantly subtle comic performance – Something the author of the book the film was based on, had huge doubts about, fearing that Presley would try too hard to be funny, rather than letting the script do the work, but his doubts were soon put to bed upon seeing Presley's intelligent and perceptive performance, showing that he fully understood the subtleties required for the role.

In Live A Little, Love A Little, 1968, he again gives us a great comedic performance, but this time he is playing a confident and successful photographer, showing that there were many facets to his skills as an actor and his ability to create a character.

Other Elvis films from the sixties that feature decent acting performances from Elvis, are Roustabout, 1964, (which also stars Barbara Stanwyck), Flaming Star, 1960, The Trouble With Girls, 1969 and Change Of Habit, 1969.

Unfortunately, his fans let him down in this area. Flocking in their millions to see the entertaining, but lightweight Blue Hawaii, 1961, (as well as making the accompanying soundtrack album the biggest selling of his lifetime), and yet the films that showcased truly excellent acting from Elvis, performed far less well at the box office, consequently trapping him into the shallow travelogues that were far beneath him.

Paradise, Hawaiian Style, 1966, has him singing to a group of dogs on a helicopter. Double Trouble 1967, features him singing Old MacDonald on the back of a truck with some chickens – and to put this into the context of the times, this was the same year The Beatles' monolithic album Sergeant Pepper's Lonely Hearts Club Band was released...

Elvis film career remains tragic waste of what could and should have been.

Elvis: Icon

"The image is one thing, a human being is another" said Elvis Presley in 1972. These words could not be any more prophetic in predicting the aftermath of Elvis' death, in which the human being became increasingly lost behind an avalanche of tacky merchandising and impersonators who completely miss the point.

Elvis impersonators succeed only in making it worse that the real one is gone. They appeal only to those shallow enough to be content with a cardboard facsimile of the real Elvis Presley. Sadly, their role in turning Elvis image into a joke and their influence in how the general public see Elvis, is so widespread that many people will never get to the real Elvis, having been put off by the false image that, in reality, bears no resemblance to the real Elvis Aron Presley.

Considering Elvis impact on music and culture, surely the man deserves better than this. Surely the man who inspired The Beatles and exposed so many new things to the world, should be better remembered as the unbelievable, unique and irreplaceable individual he was, rather than the cliched caricature perpetuated by impersonators and lazy depictions.

Of course, with any hugely successful entertainer, particularly in America, a certain amount of work is necessary in order to wade through the marketing to find the artist and to remove the commercial to find the pure music. The overuse of classic songs by The Beach Boys in commercials being a case in point – Songs that mean so much to so many, now reduced to being used to sell sneakers and soft drinks.

Thankfully, there is brilliant work being done by people like Ernst Jorgensen, who are determined to fight against the tainting of Elvis' legacy and ensure that he is remembered properly, for the irreplaceable man he was and forever will be.

Elvis undoubtedly remains an icon. Certainly *the* icon of the 20th century, but, what does this mean? An icon is a symbol. Someone who represents something. So when Elvis is referred to as an icon, what is he being said to be symbolizing? The worst excesses of a rock 'n' roll lifestyle? If there is any justice, he will symbolize the power of the individual.

When Elvis Presley walked into Sun Studios to make his first record, he surely did not do so with the intention of changing the world, but that's precisely what he did and he did it simply by being his brilliant self and that's how he deserves to be remembered.

Elvis: Pioneer

"Elvis was a blessing. They wouldn't let black music through. He opened the door for black music'. 'Elvis was an integrator. Elvis was a blessing'." – *Little Richard*

One of Elvis Presley's most significant contributions to culture, was the fact he was a non-racist in racist times. Considering that he was raised in relatively deprived and poor circumstances, this is to his credit. That he was open to all kinds of music, regardless of where it came from, is remarkable for the times in which he was raised and would have marked him out as an oddball and made him a target of the prejudice and ignorant.

Elvis made it impossible to ignore the brilliant and creative music being written and performed by black artists any longer.

There is a lazy, platitude based school of thought that says Elvis stole black music in a premeditated move in order to make himself a lot of money from it, exploiting the advantage that he was white. This itself is completely ignorant and insulting to anyone with basic intelligence. The inference is that anyone with white skin could have done it, had they only thought of it first. This, clearly is not the case. Elvis was not successful because he was white. Elvis was successful because he was Elvis Presley and undeniably brilliant.

"Describe Elvis Presley? He was the greatest who ever was, is, or will ever be'." **– Chuck Berry**

So, despite the attempts by many to make themselves look clever by dismissing Elvis as an opportunistic thief, they succeed only in displaying their ignorance.

When the 1950s establishment described Elvis as 'vulgar', this was simply veiled language. What they actually meant and feared, is that the rise of Elvis Presley would lead to racial

integration and equal rights –
A fear that was well founded.

First and foremost, Elvis was a music fan, with a vast knowledge of music of all kinds. His biggest selling single of his career was It's Now Or Never, which was based on the tune of O Sole Mio – Yet, you never hear these people complaining that he stole Italian music.

If Elvis was a copyist, how come there has never been anyone like him, before or since?

Elvis: Addict

Elvis Presley was deeply addicted to toxins. Be it in junk food or prescribed drugs. Sadly, raised on poor diet and getting nothing like the requisite nutrients for physical and mental wellbeing, the rot was set in almost from the start. When a person is not getting what they need from food, they seek it elsewhere and only find manufactured facsimiles of what nature has already provided. So, a profoundly unhappy Elvis, sought out an increasingly deadly spiral downwards, in a losing battle to try and block out the deep lows. It's easy to imagine Elvis being diagnosed with bipolar in this day and age, but far less was understood about such conditions during Elvis' lifetime.

Linda Thompson, Elvis' girlfriend during the 1970s, related that Elvis ate the same meal – meatloaf, mash potato and chowder peas – every night for at least a year. She said this was indicative of an addictive personality and while that is an undoubtedly plausible notion, it also suggests a deeply unhappy man looking to find solace in simple comforts.

Are his behaviours so unusual for someone who is so isolated, with a lot of money and having endured one crashing disappointment after another? He was getting no satisfaction from his film career during the sixties, so it was inevitable that he would throw himself into new found passions – horse riding, karate, motorcycles – as well as trying to find deeper meaning through reading spiritual books and surely it was inevitable that he would ask the question "Why me?"

Elvis: History

In a hundred years time, what will the name Elvis Presley mean? If justice prevails, the superficial things – the junk food, the jump suits, the medication – will be a mere footnote and Elvis will be remembered as the most significant artist in the history of popular music, as well as a man who made a huge and positive impact on culture, in terms of breaking down barriers and restrictions. He will stand along with The Beatles as *the* cultural icons of the 20th Century.

It becomes increasingly important to remember Elvis and The Beatles in a world in which their work is rapidly being undone in a culture where integrity is an obsolete word. Where music is controlled and sold by self-obsessed entrepreneurs with the sole purpose of making money. Where things are kept on a mediocre level so that the public are conditioned to be content with mediocrity.

It would be beneficial for mankind if more people could aspire to all the very best qualities of Elvis Presley – individuality, originality, sincerity, generosity, integrity.

Elvis' death at the age of 42, becomes more of a tragedy as time goes by, because we are left in a world with no Elvis, so we are not even afforded the consolation of having at least one Elvis on a plate full of Kardashians. The rise of such people, perhaps only goes to show that the general public never really deserved Elvis Presley, or indeed The Beatles, as it turns out they are perfectly content with the nonentities lining up to be the next puppet on reality shows, designed to make rich men richer.

On the other hand, considering the amount of mediocrity we are subjected to today, it is all the more remarkable that the world ever had an Elvis Presley and that is something for which we must be eternally grateful.

Elvis Presley

1935 – 1977

Made in the USA
Columbia, SC
06 June 2025

59039864R00046